chillies

chillies

Great recipe ideas with a classic ingredient

>> in 60 ways

APPLE

First published in the UK in 2008 by
Apple Press
7 Greenland Street
London NW1 0ND
United Kingdom
www.apple-press.com

ISBN: 978-1-84543-256-0

Editors: Sylvy Soh, Yong Kim Siang
Designer: Bernard Go Kwang Meng
Photography: Jambu Studio

Limits of Liability/Disclaimer of Warranty: The Author and Publisher of
this book have used their best efforts in preparing this book. The Publisher
makes no representation or warranties with respect to the contents of this
book and is not responsible for the outcome of any recipe in this book.
While the Publisher has reviewed each recipe carefully, the reader may
not always achieve the results desired due to variations in ingredients,
cooking temperatures and individual cooking abilities. The Publisher
shall in no event be liable for any loss of profit or any other commercial
damage, including but not limited to special, incidental, consequential, or
other damages.

Other Marshall Cavendish Offices:
Marshall Cavendish Ltd. 119 Wardour Street, London W1F 0UW, UK •
Marshall Cavendish Corporation. 99 White Plains Road, Tarrytown NY
10591-9001, USA • Marshall Cavendish International (Thailand) Co Ltd.
253 Asoke, 12th Flr, Sukhumvit 21 Road, Klongtoey Nua, Wattana, Bangkok
10110, Thailand • Marshall Cavendish (Malaysia) Sdn Bhd, Times Subang,
Lot 46, Subang Hi-Tech Industrial Park, Batu Tiga, 40000 Shah Alam,
Selangor Darul Ehsan, Malaysia

Marshall Cavendish is a trademark of Times Publishing Limited

Printed in Singapore by Utopia Press Pte Ltd

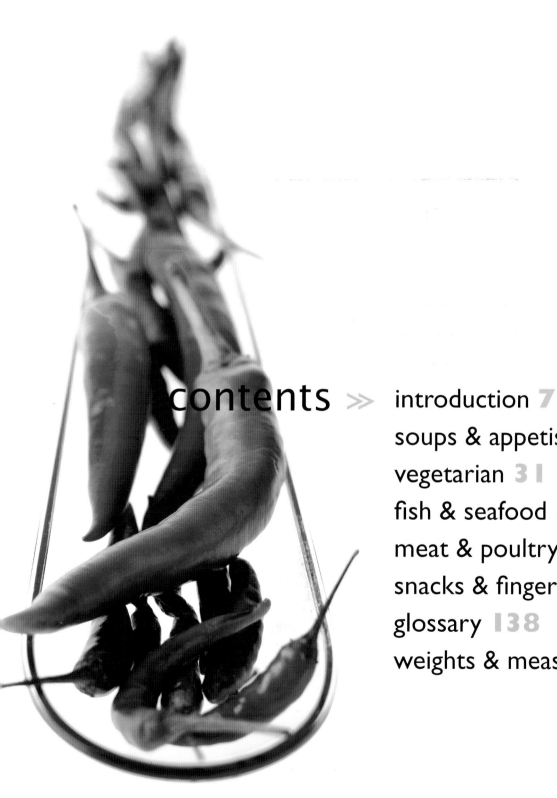

contents »

introduction >>

For the uninitiated, chillies are often abhorred as they burn the tongue and render one's taste buds numb. However, the inaugural fiery sensation is but a prelude to the amazing depth, and variety of taste and spiciness that chillies potentially provide to food.

Chillies play an important role in many world cuisines. According to historical and archaeological evidence, chillies were first cultivated by prehistoric people residing in various areas in North and South America. The Spanish, who were at that point of time prominent seafaring traders, also introduced chillies into various cultures around the world, such as India, China, Korea and the Philippines. As a result of such trade, chillies are now cultivated as a prime produce in various countries around the world.

Chillies are amazingly versatile. In their simplest form, chillies are used for spicing up a dish through their flavour and colour. However, they can be employed in countless different ways, especially when it comes to different cultural cuisines. In Mexico, chillies are consumed as a part of relishes and dips, an example being the classic chilli con carne, a spicy meat-based bean dip. Various Mediterranean dishes consist of grilled and blackened capsicums for their smoky, sweet flavour. In Asian countries, chillies are typically used to add flavour and spice. Bird's eye chillies feature as an ubiquitous part of Thai cuisine and are used in dipping sauces, curries, soups and meat dishes. Capsicums, or sweet bell peppers have a sweet and refreshing zing that add plenty of flavour to Chinese stir-fried dishes. Chillies and capsicums can also be used as part of a creative dish presentation, whether as a garnish or as a food container. Some chilli varieties featured are also available in pickled, powdered or dried form.

Appreciating chillies might take time and effort, but with plenty of perseverance, one will not be disappointed as they wend their way into your diet, and heart.

Nutrional Content

Chillies are rich in vitamins A and C. Capsicums contain a high amount of B vitamins, and red capsicums in particular contain a high amount of beta carotene, an anti-oxidant that is believed to prevent cancer. Chillies and capsicum also contain an ingredient called capsaicin, which is employed in various homeopathic treatments and in relieving bodily aches and pains.

Choosing And Storing Chillies

Chillies and capsicums should be bright in colour, firm to the touch, and unblemished, with a fresh, sharp smell. Fresh chillies and capsicums can be stored in the crisper section of the refrigerator, where they can keep for up to 2 weeks. Good quality chilli in powdered form should be fragrant and a deep, rich colour.

soups & appetisers

red capsicum and tomato soup

This light and creamy soup is refreshingly tasty.
Serves 4

Ingredients

Red capsicum (bell pepper)	1, medium, cored, seeded and halved
Olive oil	1 Tbsp
Garlic	1 clove, peeled and crushed
Onion	1, small, peeled and finely chopped
Potato	1, peeled and diced
Tomatoes	450 g (1 lb), peeled and seeded
Tomato purée	1 Tbsp
Water	275 ml (9$\frac{1}{3}$ fl oz / 1$\frac{1}{5}$ cups
Fresh basil	15 g ($\frac{1}{2}$ oz)
Salt	to taste
Plain natural yoghurt	225 g (8 oz)
Cucumber	$\frac{1}{2}$, peeled, cored and cut lengthwise

Method

- Sear capsicum in a grill pan over high heat until skin blackens. Transfer to a plastic or polythene bag, seal and leave to cool. Peel, chop finely and set aside.

- Heat oil in a large saucepan over medium heat. Stir-fry garlic until fragrant. Add onion and stir-fry until soft.

- Add capsicum, potato, tomatoes, tomato purée, water and half of the basil leaves. Cover and simmer for 15–20 minutes, or until potato has softened. Set aside to cool.

- Pour mixture into a blender (food processor). Add salt, yoghurt, cucumber and remaining basil leaves and blend until fine.

- Transfer soup to a saucepan and bring to the boil over medium heat for 3 minutes. Garnish as desired and serve immediately.

spicy pickled vegetables

Known as acar in Malay, these pickled vegetables are great as a pre-dinner snack or as a side dish.

Makes about 1.2 kg (2 lb 10 oz)

Ingredients

Cucumbers	1.25 kg (2 lb 9 oz), halved lengthwise, cored and cut into 3.5-cm (1½-in) long strips
Carrot	1, peeled and cut into 3.5-cm (1½-in) long strips
Salt	30 g (1 oz)
Vinegar	300 ml (10 fl oz / 1¼ cups)
Long beans	300 g (10½ oz), cut into 3.5-cm (1½-in)
Cabbage	600 g (1 lb 5 oz), cut into 2.5-cm (1-in) pieces
Red chillies	4, seeded and cut into thin strips
Cooking oil	150 ml (5 fl oz / ⅔ cup)
Sugar	150 g (5⅓ oz)
Peanuts	200 g (7 oz) roasted and coarsely ground

Seasoning

Dried chillies	20, soaked
Red chillies	6
Shallots	360 g (12⅔ oz), peeled
Garlic	1 bulb, peeled
Turmeric	2.5-cm (1-in) knob, peeled
Galangal	2.5-cm (1-in) knob, peeled
Candlenuts	3

Method

- Place cucumber and carrot strips in a mixing bowl. Add 1 Tbsp of salt, mix well and leave for 30 minutes.
- Rinse cucumber and carrot strips thoroughly and drain well. Pat dry with paper towels, absorbing as much water as possible.
- Half-fill a saucepan with water. Add 180 ml (6 fl oz / ¾ cup) vinegar and bring to the boil. Blanch cucumber and carrot strips, long beans, cabbage and red chillies. Transfer to a colander and drain well.
- Arrange vegetables in a single layer on a large tray and sun them for 30 minutes.
- Prepare seasoning. Combine all seasoning ingredients in a blender (food processor), blend into a paste and set aside.
- Heat oil in a wok over medium heat. Stir-fry seasoning paste until fragrant. Add remaining vinegar, sugar and salt. Combine with pickled vegetables and peanuts and mix well.
- Cover pickled vegetables and leave overnight for flavours to infuse. Store in two 600 g glass containers and refrigerate.
- Serve chilled.

flour tortillas with chilli salsa

This hot and tangy chilli salsa dip is excellent not only with flour tortillas, but also with corn chips or vegetable sticks.

Serves 4–6

Ingredients

Chilli Salsa Dip

Tomatoes	4, medium-size, finely chopped
Green chillies	4, seeded and finely chopped
Red chilli	1, seeded and finely chopped
Garlic	2 cloves, peeled and minced
Vinegar or lime juice	2 Tbsp
Vegetable oil	4 Tbsp
Ground cumin	1/2 tsp

Flour Tortillas

Plain (all-purpose) flour	400 g (14 1/3 oz)
Salt	1/2 tsp
Baking powder	1/2 tsp
Vegetable shortening or lard	3 Tbsp
Warm water	125 ml (4 fl oz / 1/2 cup)

Method

- Prepare salsa dip. Combine salsa ingredients in a bowl and mix well. Refrigerate for at least 2 hours.

- Prepare tortillas. Sift flour, salt and baking powder into a large mixing bowl. Add shortening or lard. Use the back of a fork or pastry cutter to cut in the shortening or lard.

- Add water a little at a time, kneading mixture into a soft dough. Dough should not be sticky. Add more warm water if necessary.

- Divide dough into 6 portions and leave to rest for 10 minutes. Dust a work surface with flour, then roll each portion into a thin circle about 10 cm (4 in) in diameter.

- Heat a cast iron pan over medium heat. Cook tortillas for about 30 seconds on each side, or until brown spots appear. Cover tortillas with a towel to keep warm.

- Serve tortillas warm, with chilli salsa dip on the side.

tempura

Piman is the Japanese name for capsicum (bell peppers), but this particular variety is small and thin. Their crisp flesh and aroma works well deep-fried.

Serves 2–4

Ingredients

Tempura Batter

Egg yolk	1
Ice cold water	200 ml (6½ fl oz / 4/5 cup)
Plain (all-purpose) flour	125 g (4½ oz)
Piman peppers	2, seeded and cut into quarters
Sweet potato	1, peeled and cut lengthwise into thick slices
Prawns (shrimps)	6, peeled and deveined, leaving tails intact
Cooking oil for deep frying	

Condiments

Japanese soy sauce (*shoyu*)
Finely grated white radish (daikon)

Method

- Prepare tempura batter. In a large mixing bowl, combine egg yolk with water and mix well. Gradually fold flour into egg yolk mixture and do not over mix. The batter should still be lumpy.

- Pat vegetables and prawns dry with paper towels. Make 3 slits on the belly side of each prawn to keep them straight while frying.

- Heat oil in a large frying pan over high heat. Dip vegetables and prawns in batter and fry in batches until golden in colour. Drain well.

- Serve hot with Japanese soy sauce (*shoyu*) and grated white radish (daikon) on the side.

 NOTE

Tempura is usually consumed alongside a staple, such as udon (thick wheat noodles), soba (buckwheat noodles), or Japanese rice.

orange and capsicum soup

This soup is low in fat and can even be made healthier if the fat in the chicken stock is skimmed off before use.

Serves 4

Ingredients

Yellow capsicums (bell peppers)	2, cored, seeded and halved
Green capsicums (bell peppers)	2, cored, seeded and halved
Orange	1, large
Onion	1, large, peeled and finely chopped
Chicken stock	350 ml (11¾ fl oz / 1⅓ cups)
Salt	to taste
Ground black pepper	to taste
Black olives	4, pitted and quartered

Method

- Preheat oven to 180°C (350°F). Place capsicums on a baking tray and cook under the grill for 10 minutes, or until skins are blackened. Transfer to a plastic or polythene bag, seal and leave to cool. Peel and discard blackened skin, chop capsicum finely and set aside.

- Grate half the orange for zest, then squeeze to extract juice. Slice remaining zest into fine strips. Set aside.

- Bring orange juice to the boil in a saucepan over medium heat. Add onion, cover and simmer for 10 minutes or until onion is soft. Remove from heat and set aside to cool.

- Using a blender (food processor), blend cooled mixture with capsicums, orange zest and chicken stock.

- Return mixture to the saucepan and simmer over low heat for 5 minutes while stirring constantly. Season with salt and black pepper. Garnish with olives and orange peel strips. Serve immediately.

burritos with chilli pepper filling

Burritos are traditionally eaten in South American cuisine. This version is spicy and delicious.

Serves 4

Ingredients

Flour tortillas (see p 14)	4, large, 30 cm (12 in) in diameter
Chilli sauce	4 Tbsp
Lettuce	2 leaves, shredded
Low fat Cheddar cheese	100 g (3½ oz), shredded

Filling

Olive oil	2 Tbsp
Garlic	1 clove, peeled and finely chopped
Onion	1, large, peeled and finely chopped
Jalapeño pepper	1, seeded and diced
Tomato	1, large, seeded and diced
Red chilli	1, seeded and finely chopped
Tomato sauce	2 Tbsp

Method

- Prepare filling. Heat oil in a frying pan over medium heat. Stir-fry garlic and onion until fragrant. Add jalapeño pepper, tomato, chilli and tomato sauce. Stir-fry for 2–3 minutes and set aside.

- Divide fillling into 4 portions. Spread 1 Tbsp of chilli sauce in the centre of a tortilla. Spoon 1 portion of filling onto chilli sauce, then top with shredded lettuce and cheese.

- Fold one edge of tortilla over filling, tuck in the sides and roll up. Repeat steps for remaining tortillas.

- Serve warm.

anchovy sambal

(sambal ikan bilis)

A sambal is a condiment or side dish made using chillies, and is popularly used to spice up a meal in Southeast Asia.

Serves 4

Ingredients

Dried anchovies (*ikan bilis*)	150 g (5⅓ oz), soaked for 10 minutes, then drained
Red chillies	3
Dried chillies	5, soaked in warm water for 15 minutes, then drained
Ginger	5-cm (2-in) knob, peeled and shredded
Dried prawn (shrimp) paste (*belacan*)	1 tsp
Lemon grass	1 stalk, hard outer leaves removed
Turmeric	3.5-cm (1½-in) knob, peeled
Shallots	8, peeled and sliced
Garlic	3 cloves, peeled and sliced
Cooking oil	5 Tbsp
Tamarind pulp	1 Tbsp, dissolved in 100 ml (3⅓ fl oz / ⅜ cup) of water and strained
Sugar	to taste
Salt	to taste

Method

- Discard anchovy heads, if desired. Rinse in water, then clean and drain. Set aside.

- Combine chillies, ginger, dried prawn paste, lemon grass, turmeric, shallots and garlic in a blender (food processor), and blend into a fine paste.

- Heat oil in a frying pan over medium heat and stir-fry paste until fragrant. Add anchovies and stir-fry for 1 minute, then add tamarind juice gradually, stirring consistently until gravy thickens.

- Add sugar and salt to taste. Stir-fry for a few minutes more before removing from heat. Serve as a relish with rice dishes.

NOTE

Fresh anchovies can be used, if available.

cream of jalapeño soup

Creamy and tangy, this soup is perfect as an appetiser or light meal.
Serves 4

Ingredients

Olive oil	1/2 Tbsp
Butter	2 Tbsp, melted
Spanish onions	2, peeled and cut into small cubes
Garlic	4 cloves, peeled and minced
Jalapeño peppers	7, seeded and finely chopped
Tomatoes	2, peeled and cut into small cubes
Double(heavy) cream	1.5 litres (48 fl oz / 6 cups)
Salt	to taste
Ground black pepper	to taste

Method

- Heat oil in a large saucepan over medium heat. Add butter, onions and garlic and stir-fry for 1 minute, or until onions are translucent. Add jalapeño peppers and lower heat.

- Add tomatoes and cream and simmer for 20 minutes. Stir consistently to prevent liquid from burning. Remove from heat and season with salt and black pepper.

- Serve immediately.

tom yam soup

The combination of spicy and sour flavours in this popular Thai favourite awakens one's taste buds. Simply remove the seeds of the chillies if a less spicy dish is desired.

Serves 4

Ingredients

Fish or seafood stock	1.25 litres (40 fl oz / 5 cups)
Galangal	2.5-cm (1-in) knob, peeled and sliced
Lemon grass	2 stalks, cut into 2.5-cm (1-in) lengths
Kaffir lime leaves	5
Red bird's eye chillies	10, chopped
Red chilli	1, chopped
Button mushrooms	8, halved
Prawns (shrimps)	10, medium, peeled
Fish fillet (eg. cod, mullet, snapper)	150 g (5$\frac{1}{3}$ oz), cut into thick slices
Lime juice	4 Tbsp
Fish sauce	1 Tbsp
Salt	to taste
Ground white pepper	to taste
Coriander (cilantro) leaves	

Method

- Place stock in a pot. Add galangal, lemon grass, kaffir lime leaves and chillies, then bring to the boil for 10 minutes, or until stock has reduced by one-third.

- Add button mushrooms, prawns, fish slices, lime juice and fish sauce. Return stock to the boil and add salt and pepper to taste. Taste and add more lime juice if desired.

- Serve hot, garnished with coriander leaves.

kimchi

This spicy side dish is consumed by Koreans daily and is the perfect complement to a bowl of plain white rice.

Makes 500 g

Ingredients

Chinese (napa) cabbage	1 kg (2 lb 3 oz), coarsely chopped
Kosher or pickling salt (non-iodised)	3 Tbsp
Cold water	375 ml (12 fl oz / 1½ cups)
Spring onions (scallions)	4, finely chopped
Ginger	5-cm (2-in) knob, peeled and grated
Dried chilli flakes	1½ tsp
Garlic	4 cloves, peeled and finely chopped
Chilli powder	2 tsp

Method

- Place cabbage and salt in a large mixing bowl and mix well. Use a smaller bowl or plate to weigh down cabbage. Set aside for 3 hours at room temperature. Toss the cabbage occasionally during this period.

- Rinse cabbage with cold water, drain and squeeze out as much water as possible.

- Place cabbage and remaining ingredients in an airtight container and mix well. Set aside for 2–3 days in a cool place. Store refrigerated.

NOTE

To achieve a fully fermented kimchi, you can also opt to put it in a jar and leave for 3–7 days at room temperature. Store refrigerated.

vegetarian

grilled capsicums and vegetables

Reminiscent of typical Mediterranean fare, this simple and refreshing salad is also colourful and attractive.

Serves 2–4

Ingredients

Red capsicums (bell peppers)	2, cored, seeded and halved
Yellow capsicums (bell peppers)	2, cored, seeded and halved
Courgettes (zucchinis)	2, cut into small cubes
Cherry tomatoes	225 g (8 oz), halved
Black olives	12, pitted
Walnuts (optional)	2 Tbsp, chopped

Dressing

Pesto	1 Tbsp
Olive oil	2 Tbsp
Balsamic vinegar	1 Tbsp

Method

- Sear capsicums in a grill pan over high heat until skins are blackened. Transfer to a plastic or polythene bag, seal and leave to cool. Peel skins and discard. Cut capsicums into squares.

- Prepare salad. Place capsicums, courgettes, tomatoes and olives into a salad bowl. Set aside.

- Prepare dressing. Place dressing ingredients in a mixing bowl and mix well. Drizzle over salad.

- Garnish with chopped walnuts, if desired.

chunky capsicum salad

Fragrant and flavourful, the thick capsicum slices combine perfectly with warm bread for a simple meal.

Serves 4

Ingredients

Green capsicums (bell peppers)	2, cored, seeded and halved
Red capsicums (bell peppers)	2, cored, seeded and halved
Extra virgin olive oil	6 Tbsp
Garlic	2 cloves, peeled and crushed
Chopped fresh rosemary	4 Tbsp
Chopped fresh thyme	4 Tbsp
Red wine vinegar	2 Tbsp
Black olives	4, pitted and sliced
White bread	2 thick slices, toasted, crusts removed and cut into 1-cm (1/2 in) cubes

Method

- Cut capsicums into thick slices.
- Heat oil in a large frying pan over medium heat. Add garlic and stir-fry until fragrant.
- Add sliced capsicums, rosemary and thyme. Stir-fry for 10 minutes or until capsicums are softened. Remove from heat. Add red wine vinegar and olives and toss lightly.
- Serve warm with toast on the side.

fig and chilli tagliatelle

The combination of figs and chillies livens up this lemony, creamy pasta.
Serves 4

Ingredients

Lemons	2
Double (heavy) cream	125 ml (4 fl oz / $\frac{1}{2}$ cup)
Egg/spinach tagliatelle	350 g (12$\frac{1}{3}$ oz)
Extra virgin olive oil	2 Tbsp
Black figs	8, finely sliced
Salt	to taste
Ground black pepper	to taste
Cayenne pepper	1 tsp
Dried chillies	2, finely chopped
Parmesan cheese	55 g (2 oz), grated

Method

- Grate zest of both lemons into a mixing bowl. Squeeze juice from one lemon, add double cream and mix well. Set aside.
- Bring a large saucepan of lightly salted water to the boil. Cook tagliatelle until al dente. Drain well and set aside.
- Heat oil in a large frying pan over medium heat. Add figs and stir-fry for about 3 minutes, until completely caramelised.
- Add salt and black pepper to taste, then add cayenne pepper and dried chillies. Mix well.
- Pour lemon cream mixture onto pasta and mix well. Divide pasta into 4 equal portions on serving plates. Spoon figs and chillies over each portion. Serve with grated Parmesan cheese.

NOTE

Vary the amount of dried chillies to taste.

roasted vegetables in red wine

This roasted vegetable dish is so flavourful, it can be consumed as a main meal if quantities are doubled. Serve with warm, crusty bread if desired.

Serves 4

Ingredients

Aubergine (eggplant / brinjal)	1, cut into 5-cm (2-in) cubes
Salt	2 Tbsp
Shallots	8, peeled and halved
Red capsicum (bell pepper)	1, cored, seeded and cut into thick slices
Yellow capsicum (bell pepper)	1, cored, seeded and cut into thick slices
Olive oil	4 Tbsp
Red wine	4 Tbsp

Seasoning

Salt	to taste
Ground white pepper	to taste
Soft dark brown sugar	2 tsp
Chopped fresh rosemary	4 Tbsp
Chopped fresh thyme	4 Tbsp

Method

- Place aubergine in a colander and sprinkle with salt to purge the bitter juices. Leave to drain for an hour, then rinse and pat dry with a tea towel.
- Place aubergine, shallots and capsicums in a large mixing bowl. Drizzle in olive oil and toss well. Transfer to an ovenproof dish or roasting tin.
- Pour red wine over vegetables and sprinkle over seasoning ingredients. Toss well.
- Roast in a preheated oven at 220°C (440°F) for 15 minutes. Flip the vegetables over and roast for another 15 minutes. Remove and serve hot.

spicy mixed vegetables

This South Indian-inspired vegetable dish is commonly served as an accompaniment to main meals in Malaysia.

Serves 4–6

Ingredients

Vegetable oil	1 Tbsp
Green chillies	2, seeded and diced
Red chilli	1, seeded and diced
Carrot	1, peeled and sliced
Cauliflower	140 g (5 oz) cut into florets
French beans	6, tailed and halved
Aubergine (eggplant / brinjal)	1, cut into rectangular pieces about 5-cm (2-in) long
Salt	to taste
Water	625 ml (20 fl oz / 2½ cups)
Plain natural yoghurt	175 g (6 oz)
Grated coconut	200 g (7 oz)

Spices

Coriander seeds	2 tsp, crushed
Cumin seeds	1 tsp, crushed
Ground turmeric	½ tsp

Garnish

Red chilli	1, seeded and cut into long strips
Coriander leaves (cilantro)	

Method

- Heat oil in a saucepan over medium heat. Add chillies and spices. Stir-fry for 1–2 minutes.

- Add carrot, cauliflower and french beans and stir-fry until slightly soft. Add aubergine and stir-fry for 1–2 minutes.

- Add salt to taste, then add water. Lower heat and simmer for 4–5 minutes.

- Stir in yoghurt and grated coconut. Simmer for another 2 minutes, then remove from heat. Serve garnished with red chilli strips and coriander leaves.

baked golden pasta

Hearty and filling, this baked pasta dish is too simple and delicious to pass over when needing a quick yet satisfying dinner!

Serves 4

Ingredients

Olive oil	2 Tbsp
Penne	350 g (12⅓ oz)
Red capsicum (bell pepper)	1, cored seeded and thinly sliced
Green capsicum (bell pepper)	1, cored, seeded and thinly sliced
Button mushrooms	100 g (3½ oz), thinly sliced

Sauce

Butter	25 g (¾ oz)
Plain (all-purpose) flour	25 g (¾ oz)
Milk	250 ml (8 fl oz / 1 cup)
Mature Cheddar cheese	150 g (5⅓ oz), grated
Frozen peas	50 g (2 oz)
Salt	to taste
Ground black pepper	to taste

Method

- Bring a large saucepan of salted water to the boil. Add 1 Tbsp olive oil, then add penne and cook until al dente. Drain well and set aside.

- Heat remaining olive oil in a frying pan over medium heat. Add capsicums and stir-fry until slightly soft. Add mushrooms and stir-fry for 1–2 minutes, remove from heat and set aside.

- Prepare sauce. Melt butter in a saucepan over low heat. Add flour and stir until well mixed. Increase to medium heat. Gradually add milk and blend, stirring constantly until mixture boils and thickens. Stir in half of Cheddar cheese portion and add peas, salt and pepper. Allow to cook for 1 more minute and remove from heat.

- Preheat oven at 200°C (400°F). Combine pasta and vegetables in a ovenproof dish. Pour sauce over and sprinkle with remaining cheese. Bake until cheese melts.

- Serve hot.

fragrant sesame stir-fry

Sesame seeds add extra crunch and texture to this colourful, fragrant stir-fry.

Serves 4

Ingredients

Olive oil	2 Tbsp
Red bird's eye chilli	1, seeded and finely chopped
Ginger	2.5-cm (1-in) knob, peeled and finely chopped
Star anise	1
Onion	1, small peeled and finely chopped
Baby corn	4
Long beans	100 g (3½ oz)
Red, yellow and green capsicums (bell peppers)	3, medium, cored, seeded and cut into thin slices
Button mushrooms	100 g (3½ oz), thinly sliced
White sesame seeds	2 Tbsp, toasted
Corn flour (cornstarch)	1 tsp, mixed with 1 Tbsp water
Sesame oil	1 tsp

Method

- Heat olive oil in a wok over medium heat. Stir-fry chilli for 30 seconds to flavour the oil. Add ginger, star anise and onion and stir-fry until fragrant.

- Add corn, long beans and capsicums. Stir-fry until soft. Add mushrooms, 1 Tbsp sesame seeds and corn flour mixture. Stir-fry until gravy thickens. Remove and discard star anise.

- Dish out onto a serving plate and sprinkle with remaining sesame seeds. Drizzle sesame oil over and mix well. Serve immediately.

spicy cauliflower with garlic

A spicy Italian recipe that presents the humble cauliflower in a refreshing new style.

Serves 4

Ingredients

Cauliflower	350 g (12$^1/_3$ oz), cut into florets
Olive oil	4 Tbsp
Garlic	1 clove, peeled and crushed
Red chilli	2, seeded and finely chopped
Black olives	8, pitted and halved
Breadcrumbs	4 Tbsp
Salt	to taste
Ground black pepper	to taste

Method

- Bring a pot of lightly salted water to the boil. Blanch cauliflower for 3 minutes, then drain and set aside.

- Heat oil in a frying pan over medium heat. Add garlic, chilli and cauliflower. Stir-fry for 3 minutes or until fragrant. Add olives, breadcrumbs and salt and black pepper to taste. Stir-fry for another minute and remove from heat.

- Serve immediately.

red cabbage, carrot and piman pepper salad

The piman peppers add spice to this colourful, summery salad.
Serves 4–6

Ingredients

Red cabbage	4 large leaves
Carrots	2, peeled and cut into long strips
Piman peppers	2, seeded and cut into thin strips
Red onion	1, peeled and chopped
Red chilli	1, seeded and finely chopped

Dressing

Red wine vinegar	1 Tbsp
Balsamic vinegar	2 Tbsp
Garlic	1 clove, peeled and finely chopped
Salt	to taste
Ground black pepper	to taste
Extra virgin olive oil	4 Tbsp

Method

- Cut 2 cabbage leaves into long strips. Combine with carrots, peppers, onion and chilli in a mixing bowl and toss lightly.
- Arrange remaining red cabbage leaves on a serving dish. Spoon in mixed vegetables and chill in the refrigerator for 1 hour.
- Prepare dressing. Combine dressing ingredients in a mixing bowl and mix well.
- Serve salad with dressing on the side.

fusili salad with capsicums and parsley

This light, refreshing salad flavoured with parsley is perfect for a quick lunch if one is rushed for time.

Serves 4

Ingredients

Salt	to taste
Olive oil	1 Tbsp
Fusili	400 g (14⅓ oz)
Red capsicum	1, large, cored, seeded and thinly sliced
Yellow capsicum	1, large, cored, seeded and thinly sliced
Cherry tomatoes	4, sliced
Black olives	4, pitted and finely chopped
Grated Parmesan cheese	

Dressing

Olive oil	90 ml (3 fl oz / ⅜ cup)
Garlic	2 cloves, peeled and minced
Finely chopped parsley	3 Tbsp
Salt	to taste
Ground black pepper	to taste

Method

- Bring a pot of lightly salted water to the boil. Cook fusili until al dente, drain well and set aside.
- Place capsicums, tomatoes and olives in a salad bowl. Add pasta and toss well.
- Prepare dressing. Combine dressing ingredients in a mixing bowl. Pour over salad and toss well.
- Serve garnished with grated Parmesan cheese.

channa dhal with capsicums

This colourful dish originates from Gujarat, India. It has a sweet, mellow flavour and is flavoured with spices typically used in Indian cooking.

Serves 4–6

Ingredients

Channa dhal	225 g (8 oz), washed and soaked for 2 hours
Vegetable oil	4 Tbsp
Mustard seeds	1 tsp
Cumin seeds	$\frac{1}{2}$ tsp
Onion	1, peeled and finely chopped
Garlic	3 cloves, peeled and finely chopped
Ground cumin	2 tsp
Ground turmeric	$\frac{1}{2}$ tsp
Cardamom seeds	2 tsp
Salt	1$\frac{1}{2}$ tsp
Tomatoes	2, peeled and diced
Red capsicum (bell pepper)	1, cored, seeded and diced
Green capsicum (bell pepper)	1, cored, seeded and diced

Method

- Drain soaked dhal. Bring a pot of water to the boil. Add dhal and cook until soft and most of the water has been absorbed. Mash dhal lightly and set aside.

- Heat oil in a frying pan over medium–high heat. Stir-fry mustard and cumin seeds until seeds begin to pop. Add onion and stir-fry until golden brown.

- Add garlic, cumin, turmeric and cardamom seeds and stir-fry for 1 minute. Add salt and tomatoes. Stir-fry for 2 minutes.

- Add capsicums and dhal. Reduce heat and simmer for 10 minutes. Serve immediately.

crispy bean curd with spicy peanut sauce

A favourite Malay dish of crisp, golden bean curd and spicy, nutty peanut sauce.

Serves 4

Ingredients

Cooking oil for deep-frying	
Firm bean curd	4 cakes
Bean sprouts	150 g (5⅓ oz), rinsed, tailed and blanched
Cucumber	1, peeled and sliced

Peanut Sauce

Red chillies	3
Garlic	3 cloves, peeled
Tamarind pulp	1 rounded tsp, mixed with 4 Tbsp water and strained
Sugar	2 Tbsp
Peanuts	200 g (7 oz), roasted and chopped

Method

- Heat oil in a wok over medium heat. Deep-fry bean curd until light golden brown in colour. Remove bean curd, drain well and cut into quarters. Arrange on a serving dish and top with bean sprouts and cucumber. Set aside.

- Prepare peanut sauce. Place chillies, garlic, tamarind juice and sugar in a blender (food processor) and blend into a fine paste. Add peanuts and mix well.

- Ladle peanut sauce over bean curd. Serve immediately with any excess peanut sauce on the side.

fish & seafood

stir-fried squid with capsicums

Squid is perfect for stir-frying and the spicy black bean sauce makes this a tasty dish.

Serves 4

Ingredients

Squid	450 g (1 lb)
Cooking oil	3 Tbsp
Ginger	3.5-cm (1½-in) knob, peeled and finely chopped
Garlic	1 clove, peeled and finely chopped
Green chilli	1, seeded and sliced
Spring onions (scallions)	8, cut diagonally into 2.5-cm (1-in) lengths
Red capsicum (bell pepper)	1, cored, seeded and cut into 12 squares, each 2.5-cm (1-in) in length
Shiitake mushrooms	75 g (2⅔ oz), thickly sliced

Black Bean Sauce

Salted black beans	2 Tbsp, rinsed and finely chopped
Chinese cooking wine	2 Tbsp
Light soy sauce	1 Tbsp
Corn flour (cornstarch)	1 tsp
Sugar	½ tsp
Water	2 Tbsp

Method

- Clean squid. Pull away head and tentacles from body, then remove quill. Pull out entrails and peel away outer skin. Discard. Cut tentacles from head and discard rest of head. Rinse squid and cut tubes into 2-cm (1-in) rings.

- Using a pair of scissors, make 1-cm (2-in) deep cuts at 0.5 cm (¼ in) intervals all around one cut side of squid rings. This will cause the squid to curl up like a flower.

- Prepare black bean sauce. Combine sauce ingredients in a mixing bowl and mix well.

- Heat oil in a wok over medium heat. Stir-fry squid for 2 minutes, or until opaque. Remove from heat, drain and set aside.

- Add ginger, garlic and chilli to the wok and stir-fry until fragrant. Add spring onions, capsicum and mushrooms and stir-fry for 2 minutes. Add squid and black bean sauce and stir-fry for 1 minute, or until sauce thickens.

- Serve hot.

If Chinese cooking wine is not available, substitute with other rice wines or dry sherry.

grilled tuna rolls

Grilling capsicums gives them a sweet, smoky taste that goes perfectly with tuna. Rolling the capsicums is also a unique way of presenting the dish.

Serves 4–6

Ingredients

Red capsicums (bell peppers)	3, large
Canned tuna	200 g (7 oz), drained
Lemon juice	2 Tbsp
Olive oil	3 Tbsp
Green or black olives	6, pitted and chopped
Freshly chopped parsley	2 Tbsp
Celery	1 stick, finely chopped
Salt	to taste
Ground black pepper	to taste

Method

- Preheat oven to 180°C (350°F). Place capsicums on a baking tray and grill for 8–12 minutes until blackened. Transfer to a plastic or polythene bag, seal and leave to cool. Peel, halve, core and seed capsicums.

- Prepare filling. Place tuna in a small bowl and mash with a fork. Add lemon juice and oil and mix well. Add olives, parsley, celery and salt and black pepper to taste. Mix well.

- Spread out capsicums flat, with skin side down. Spoon over enough filling to fill one capsicum and roll up. Repeat for the remaining capsicum pieces.

- Serve warm.

spicy prawn and capsicum curry

This perennial Singaporean favourite goes well with yellow noodles or plain white rice.

Serves 4

Ingredients

Prawns (shrimps)	450 g (1 lb)
Vegetable oil	7 Tbsp
Garlic	2 cloves, peeled and crushed
Shallots	12, peeled and chopped
Curry leaves	1 sprig
Ground ginger	1½ Tbsp
Curry powder	3 Tbsp
Salt	to taste
Tomatoes	255 g (9 oz), chopped
Corn flour (cornstarch)	1 Tbsp, mixed with 2 Tbsp water
Coconut milk	250 ml (8 fl oz / 1 cup)
Green capsicum (bell pepper)	1, cored, seeded and cut into small squares
Cucumber	1, peeled and cut into small squares
Red chillies	2, seeded and sliced
Lemon juice	1 Tbsp
Sugar	1 tsp

Method

- Shell prawns, leaving tails intact. Make a shallow slit down the back of each prawn and devein.

- Heat oil in a saucepan over medium heat. Stir-fry garlic and shallots until light brown.

- Add curry leaves, ground ginger, curry powder and salt and stir-fry until fragrant. Add tomatoes. Reduce heat and cook for 5 minutes or until tomatoes are slightly soft.

- Add corn flour mixture and stir until curry thickens. Stir in coconut milk and mix well.

- Add prawns and cook until prawns are pink in colour. Add capsicum, cucumber, red chillies, lemon juice and sugar. Cook for 3 minutes and remove from heat.

- Serve immediately.

spicy fish patties

A Sri Lankan specialty, these crispy patties are bound to be a hit with lovers of spicy food.

Serves 2–4

Ingredients

Fish fillet	450 g (1 lb), skinned
Onion	1, large, peeled and minced
Green chillies	4, seeded and minced
Curry leaves	1 sprig, finely chopped
Egg	2, beaten and separated into 2 portions
Salt	to taste
Plain (all-purpose) flour for coating	
Breadcrumbs for coating	
Cooking oil for deep-frying	

Method

- Rinse fish fillet and pat dry. Mash fillet lightly to break meat up. Place fish, onion, chillies, curry leaves, 1 egg portion and salt in a mixing bowl. Mix well.

- Divide mixture into 4–6 portions, depending on size of desired patty. Shape each portion into a round patty of medium thickness.

- Coat patties with plain flour, then dip them in the other egg portion. Make sure the entire patty is well coated with egg before coating with breadcrumbs.

- Heat oil in a wok over high heat. Deep-fry patties until golden brown in colour. Remove from heat and drain.

- Serve immediately, with chilli sauce on the side.

piri-piri prawns

When translated, 'piri-piri' means 'small chillies' and refers to a spicy Portuguese seasoning. These tangy, spicy prawns will liven up the fare at any dinner party or barbecue.

Serves 4

Ingredients

Prawns (shrimps)	20, large, peeled and deveined, leaving tail intact
Bamboo skewers	5, soaked in water for 20 minutes

Aïoli

Mayonnaise	150 ml (5 fl oz / ²/₃ cup)
Garlic	2 cloves, peeled and crushed
Dijon mustard	4 Tbsp

Seasoning Sauce

Red chilli	2, seeded and finely chopped
Paprika	¹/₂ tsp
Ground coriander	¹/₂ tsp
Garlic	1 clove, crushed
Lime juice	2 Tbsp
Olive oil	2 Tbsp
Salt	to taste
Ground black pepper	to taste

Method

- Prepare seasoning sauce. Combine seasoning ingredients in a mixing bowl and mix well.
- Add prawns to seasoning and leave to marinate in a cool place for 30 minutes.
- Prepare aïoli. Combine ingredients in a small bowl and mix well. Set aside.
- Thread marinated prawns onto skewers. Grill on a barbecue, or a preheated oven at 180°C (350°F) for 6–8 minutes. Bast with oil and turn frequently, until prawns turn pink in colour.
- Serve with aïoli on the side.

spring rolls with spicy sauce

Serve this slightly hot and gingery dish as a finger food or as part of a Chinese meal.

Serves 4–6

Ingredients

Spring roll wrappers	12
Egg	1, small, beaten
Cooking oil for deep-frying	

Spicy Sauce

Red bird's eye chillies	2, seeded and finely chopped
Dark soy sauce	2 Tbsp
Lemon juice	1 Tbsp
Shallots	2, peeled and finely sliced
Garlic	1 clove, peeled and finely chopped
Water	1 Tbsp

Filling

Vegetable oil	1 Tbsp
Sesame oil	1 Tbsp
Garlic	2 cloves, peeled and finely chopped
Shallots	2, peeled and finely chopped
Red chillies	2, seeded and finely chopped
Ginger	2.5-cm (1-in) knob, peeled and grated
Crab meat	350 g (12¹⁄₃ oz)
Chinese cabbage	6 leaves, shredded
Carrot	1, peeled and shredded
Bean sprouts	300 g (10½ oz), tailed and rinsed

Spring onions (scallions)	2, chopped
Chinese cooking wine	1 Tbsp
Light soy sauce	1 Tbsp
Salt	to taste
Ground black pepper	to taste

Method

- Prepare spicy sauce. Combine ingredients in a mixing bowl and mix well. Set aside.

- Prepare filling. Heat vegetable and sesame oil in a wok over medium heat. Stir-fry garlic, shallots, chillies and ginger until fragrant. Add crab meat, cabbage, carrot, bean sprouts and spring onions. Stir-fry until vegetables are slightly soft.

- Add Chinese cooking wine and light soy sauce and stir-fry for another minute. Add salt and black pepper to taste and remove from heat.

- Divide filling into 12 portions. Spoon a portion onto the centre of each spring roll wrapper. Fold one edge of wrapper over filling and tuck in the sides. Roll up and seal with a little water. Dip spring rolls in beaten egg.

- Heat oil over high heat. Deep-fry spring rolls until crispy and golden brown in colour. Drain well before serving.

- Serve immediately, with spicy sauce on the side.

seafood pita

This capsicum and seafood filling goes perfectly with warm, toasted pita bread.

Serves 4

Ingredients

Olive oil	2 tsp
Garlic	2 cloves, peeled and finely chopped
Onion	2, large, peeled and finely chopped
Red capsicum (bell pepper)	1, cored, seeded and cut into thin slices
Yellow capsicum (bell pepper)	1, cored, seeded and cut into thin slices
Tomato	1, seeded and diced
Prawns (shrimps)	10, small, peeled and deveined
Paprika	2 tsp
Tomato purée	4 Tbsp
Salt	to taste
Ground black pepper	to taste
Pita bread	4
Lettuce	12 leaves, finely shredded

Method

• Heat oil in a frying pan over medium heat. Stir-fry garlic and onions until fragrant. Add capsicums and stir-fry for 5 minutes.

• Add tomato and prawns and stir-fry for 1 minute. Add paprika, tomato purée, salt and black pepper. Stir-fry for another 2 minutes and reduce heat to simmer for 5–7 minutes.

• Meanwhile, toast pita bread in a preheated oven at 180°C (350°F) for 5–7 minutes. Cut each piece into half to make pockets. Spoon filling and shredded lettuce into each pocket.

• Serve immediately.

asam fish

This spicy, sweet and sour concoction is best savoured with plain white rice.

Serves 4

Ingredients

Mackerel (or any white-fleshed fish) fillet	450 g (1 lb)
Salt	1 tsp
Red chillies	8, seeded
Red bird's eye chillies	8
Lemon grass	2 stalks
Turmeric	1.25-cm (1/2-in) knob, peeled and finely chopped
Shallots	10, peeled and finely chopped
Cooking oil	2 Tbsp
Water	625 ml (20 fl oz / 2 1/2 cups)
Dried sour fruit (*asam gelugor*)	2 slices
Pineapple rings	4, cut into small pieces
Salt	1 tsp
Sugar	1 tsp

Method

- Wash fish fillet and rub with salt. Cut into 3 big pieces and set aside.

- Place chillies, lemon grass, turmeric and shallots in a blender (food processor) and blend into a fine paste.

- Heat oil in a large saucepan over high heat. Stir-fry paste until fragrant. Add water and dried sour fruit slices and bring to the boil for 3–5 minutes. Add fish, pineapple, salt and sugar. Reduce heat and simmer for 10 minutes.

- Serve hot with plain white rice.

If dried sour fruit slices are not available, replace with tamarind pulp. Dissolve 1 tsp tamarind pulp in 4 Tbsp water and strain before use.

sambal prawns and bean curd

This hot and spicy dish uses tempeh (fermented soy bean cake) which comes in rectangular packets readily available in Singapore, Malaysia and Indonesia. Reduce the chilli portions for the uninitiated!

Serves 6

Ingredients

Cooking oil for deep-frying Tempeh (fermented soy bean cake)	2 pieces, cut into small squares
Firm bean curd	300 g (10½ oz), cut into small rectangular pieces
Vegetable oil	4 Tbsp
Onion	1, large, peeled and sliced
Red chilli	1, seeded and sliced
Green chilli	1, seeded and sliced
Long beans	4, cut into short lengths
Prawns (shrimps)	450 g (1 lb), medium, peeled and deveined
Tamarind pulp	1 tsp, mixed with 4 Tbsp water and strained
Coconut milk	750 ml (24 fl oz / 3 cups)
Salt	to taste

Sambal Paste

Dried red chillies	6, soaked
Shallots	6, peeled
Garlic	3 cloves, peeled
Ground turmeric	1 tsp
Dried prawn paste (*belacan*)	2.5-cm (1-in), toasted

Method

- Heat oil in a wok over high heat. Deep-fry tempeh until light brown in colour. Remove, drain and set aside.

- Deep-fry bean curd pieces until light brown in colour. Remove, drain and set aside.

- Prepare sambal paste. Place chillies and shallots in a blender (food processor) and blend into a fine paste. Set aside.

- Heat vegetable oil over medium heat. Stir-fry onion until soft. Add sambal paste and chillies and stir-fry until fragrant.

- Add long beans, prawns, tempeh and bean curd. Stir-fry until long beans and prawns are cooked.

- Stir in tamarind juice and coconut milk. Add salt to taste and bring to the boil. Reduce heat and allow to simmer for 5–7 minutes. Serve with plain white rice.

crab balls with hot mustard dip

These crispy, fluffy crab balls are meltingly delicious, especially when savoured with a piquant hot mustard dip.

Serves 4

Ingredients

Vegetable oil	4 Tbsp
Onion	½, small, peeled and finely chopped
Ground coriander	½ tsp
Ground cumin	½ tsp
Dried oregano	1 tsp
Salt	to taste
Chilli powder	½ tsp
Paprika	½ tsp
Crab meat	225 g (8 oz)
Green chillies	2, seeded and finely chopped
Spring onions (scallions)	2, chopped
Mustard	2 Tbsp
Parmesan cheese	30 g (1 oz), grated
Dry breadcrumbs	55 g (2 oz)
Eggs	2
Ground black pepper	to taste
Plain (all-purpose) flour	100 g (3½ oz)
Cooking oil for deep-frying	

Hot Mustard Dip

Spring onions (scallions)	2, chopped
Tomato	1, seeded and chopped
Mustard	2 Tbsp

Method

- Heat oil in a frying pan over medium heat. Add onion and stir-fry for 1 minute. Add coriander, cumin, oregano, chilli powder, paprika and salt. Stir-fry until fragrant.

- Remove from heat and transfer to a large mixing bowl. Add crab meat, chillies, spring onions, mustard, cheese and 2 Tbsp breadcrumbs. Crack 1 egg into the bowl and mix well.

- Divide mixture into 8 even portions. Roll each portion into a round ball.

- Beat remaining egg with pepper to taste. Coat balls with flour and dip in egg before coating with breadcrumbs.

- Prepare dip. Combine ingredients in a blender (food processor) and blend into a fine paste. Season with salt and black pepper to taste. Set aside.

- Heat oil for deep-frying over medium heat. Deep-fry crab balls until golden brown in colour. Drain well and serve immediately, with hot mustard dip on the side.

mussel stew

A rich, spicy broth that is perfect as a light starter.
Serves 4

Ingredients

Mussels	1 kg (2 lb 3 oz)
Fish sauce	2 Tbsp
Red chilli	1, seeded and finely chopped
Green chilli	1, seeded and finely chopped
Ginger	1-cm (½-in) knob, peeled and sliced
Tabasco sauce	2 Tbsp
Sake	4 Tbsp
Spring onions (scallions)	4, cut into 2.5-cm (1-in) lengths
Salt	to taste
Ground white pepper	to taste

Method

- Soak mussels in a large basin of water for 30 minutes for them to expel any sand. Remove mussels from basin, being careful not to agitate sand at the bottom of the basin. Scrub mussels clean.

- Place 1.25 litres (40 fl oz / 5 cups) water in a pot and bring to the boil. Add fish sauce, chillies, ginger, Tabasco sauce and sake. Add mussels and reduce to low heat. Simmer for 5–7 minutes, stirring occasionally.

- Add spring onions and salt and pepper to taste. Simmer for a few minutes more and remove from heat. Discard any unopened mussels.

- Serve immediately.

chilli crabs

Lauded as the national dish of Singapore, this popular seafood dish is simpler to prepare than what one imagines.

Serves 2–4

Ingredients

Crabs	500 g (1 lb, 1½ oz)
Cooking oil	3 Tbsp
Garlic	2 cloves, peeled and finely chopped
Red chillies	2, seeded and finely chopped
Ginger	2, peeled and thinly sliced
Corn flour (cornstarch)	1 Tbsp, mixed with 2 Tbsp water
Egg	1, beaten
Chilli oil	2 Tbsp

Chilli Crab Sauce

Chilli sauce	4 Tbsp
Sugar	1 tsp
Salt	2 tsp
Water	500 ml (16 fl oz / 2 cups)

Method

- If crabs are alive, place in the freezer for a few hours. Remove and scrub crabs clean. Remove triangular flap on the underside of each crab, then pull top shell off. Remove gill filaments and rinse crabs. Cut crabs into 4 pieces, then remove pincers. Use a mallet to crack pincers. Set crabs aside.

- Prepare sauce. Combine sauce ingredients in a large mixing bowl and mix well. Set aside.

- Heat oil in a wok over medium heat. Stir-fry garlic, red chillies and ginger until fragrant. Add crabs and stir-fry until shells turn red.

- Add chilli crab sauce and bring to the boil. Reduce heat and simmer for 5–10 minutes. Add corn flour mixture. Stir gently until sauce thickens. Add egg and chilli oil and cook for 1–2 minutes.

- Serve immediately.

baked chillies with tuna

Other than adding spice, chillies can used to liven up the presentation of a dish, such as in the case of this simple but attractive meal.

Serves 4

Ingredients

Red chillies	4, large
Green chillies	4, large

Filling

Cooking oil	1 Tbsp
Onion	1, peeled and finely chopped
Curry paste	2 tsp
Canned tuna flakes	200 g (7 oz)
Potatoes	2, boiled, peeled and mashed

Method

- Seed chillies. Make a medium-length incision down the length of each chilli, leaving the stem intact. Soak in cold water to remove seeds and set aside.

- Prepare filling. Heat oil in a frying pan over medium heat and stir-fry onion until soft. Add curry paste and stir-fry until fragrant. Remove from heat.

- Combine paste with tuna flakes and mashed potatoes. Mix well. Spoon as much filling as possible into each chilli.

- Bake chillies in a preheated oven at 180°C (350°F) for 20 minutes.

- Garnish as desired and serve hot.

For a visually pleasing dish, choose plump, straight chillies that are unblemished and a deep red or green colour.

meat & poultry

cajun spiced chicken

This Cajun dish is fragrant and savoury. The blend of spices complement the flavour of chicken perfectly.

Serves 4

Ingredients

Chicken thighs	4, skinned
Garlic	2 cloves, peeled and finely chopped
Onions	2, peeled and finely chopped
Olive oil	for basting
Green capsicums (bell peppers)	2, cored, seeded and cut into thick slices
Red capsicums (bell peppers)	2, cored, seeded and cut into thick slices
Salt	to taste
Ground black pepper	to taste

Cajun Spice Seasoning

Black peppercorns	1 tsp
Fennel seeds	1 tsp
Dried oregano	1 tsp
Sage	1 tsp
Thyme	1 tsp
Rock salt	1/2 tsp
Cumin seeds	1/2 tsp
Paprika	1/2 tsp
Cayenne powder	1/2 tsp
Mustard powder	1/2 tsp

Method

* Prepare Cajun seasoning. Combine ingredients in a blender (food processor) and blend until fine. Rub chicken with seasoning, then set aside for 30 minutes.

* Place garlic and onion into a large bowl and mix well with chicken. Grease a baking tray with olive oil and arrange chicken and capsicums on it. Season with salt and pepper to taste.

* Bake in a preheated oven at 200°C (400°F) for 12–15 minutes, or until the juices run clear when the thickest part of the thigh is pierced with the tip of a knife.

* Serve immediately.

black pepper and capsicum chicken

This is a traditional Sichuan dish. Cut the chicken and capsicums into pieces of a similar size for better presentation.

Serves 4

Ingredients

Chicken breasts	400 g (14$\frac{1}{3}$ oz), cut into 2.5-cm (1-in) pieces
Corn flour	2 Tbsp
Vegetable oil	2 Tbsp
Onion	1, large, peeled and cut into small squares
Red capsicum (bell pepper)	1, seeded and cut into small squares
Green capsicum (bell pepper)	1, seeded and cut into small squares
Red chillies	2, seeded and finely chopped

Marinade

Black peppercorns	5, coarsely crushed
Light soy sauce	2 Tbsp
Salt	$\frac{1}{2}$ tsp
Sugar	$\frac{1}{2}$ tsp

Sauce

Chicken stock	4 Tbsp
Oyster sauce	1 Tbsp
Salt	to taste
Sugar	1 tsp

Method

- Prepare marinade. Combine ingredients in a mixing bowl and mix well. Add chicken and leave to marinate for 30 minutes.

- Coat chicken lightly with corn flour. Set excess cornflour aside. Heat oil in a frying pan over medium heat and stir-fry chicken until light brown. Drain well and set aside. Set frying pan aside.

- Prepare sauce. Combine all ingredients in a small bowl and mix well.

- Reheat frying pan over medium heat. Add onion and stir-fry until soft. Add capsicums and chillies and stir-fry for 2–3 minutes. Add sauce and bring mixture to the boil while stirring constantly. Add chicken and remaining corn flour, mixed with 1 Tbsp of water. Stir until gravy thickens and remove from heat.

- Serve immediately.

pickled pepper and parma ham toast

Smoky parma ham and spicy jalapeño peppers make a great combination for this simple tea-time snack.

Serves 4

Ingredients

Ciabatta bread	2 slices
Parma ham	4 slices
Pickled jalapeño peppers	4, sliced
Mozzarella cheese	75 g (2$\frac{2}{3}$ oz), sliced
Ground black pepper	to taste
Basil leaves	

Method

- Preheat oven to 180°C (350°F).
- Cut ciabatta across horizontally to get 4 flat slices of bread.
- Arrange parma ham and jalapeño peppers on each slice of bread. Top with mozzarella, then place in oven for 5 minutes, or until mozzarella has melted.
- Season with pepper to taste and garnish with basil leaves. Serve immediately.

beef kebabs with chilli and olive salsa

These spicy beef kebabs are deliciously tender and juicy, whether barbecued or baked.

Serves 4

Ingredients

Beef steaks	600 g (1 lb 5^1/$_3$ oz), cut into 4-cm (1^1/$_2$-in) cubes
Bay leaves	8
Bamboo or metal skewers	4

Chilli And Olive Salsa

Onion	1, small, peeled and finely chopped
Tomato	4, peeled, seeded and finely chopped
Black and green olives	175 g (6 oz), pitted and roughly chopped
Red chilli	1, seeded and finely chopped
Olive oil	2 Tbsp

Marinade

Garlic	2 cloves, peeled and finely chopped
Lemon juice	4 Tbsp
Olive oil	2 Tbsp
Dried chilli	1, soaked to soften, then seeded and finely chopped
Ground cumin	1 tsp
Ground coriander	1 tsp

Method

• Prepare marinade. Combine marinade ingredients in a mixing bowl and mix well. Add beef and leave to marinate for 2 hours.

• Prepare salsa. Combine ingredients in a mixing bowl and mix well. Chill in the refrigerator for 1 hour.

• Divide marinated beef cubes into 4 portions. Thread them using the skewers, alternating with the bay leaves. Use 2 bay leaves per skewer. Grill kebabs over a barbecue or in a preheated oven at 220°C (440°F) for 10–15 minutes. Turn beef skewers every 5 minutes.

• Serve immediately with salsa on the side.

stuffed capsicums

Capsicums make pretty yet edible containers for a hearty beef filling. Serve on its own as a light meal, or with other dishes for a more substantial and hearty meal.

Serves 4

Ingredients

Red capsicums (bell peppers)	4, large
Olive oil	4 Tbsp
Minced beef	450 g (1 lb)
Onion	1, peeled and finely chopped
Celery sticks	1, finely chopped
Yellow capsicum (bell pepper)	1, large, cored, seeded and finely chopped
Button mushrooms	50 g (2 oz)
Ground cinnamon	to taste
Salt	to taste
Ground black pepper	to taste
Parsley	a few sprigs

Method

- Cut caps off red capsicums. Use a spoon to scoop out seeds and cores. If necessary, cut a sliver off the base of each capsicum to make sure they stand level. Set aside.

- Prepare filling. Heat 3 Tbsp oil in a saucepan over medium heat. Sauté minced beef for 5 minutes or until cooked. Remove and set aside.

- Using the same pan, reheat the oil over medium heat. Stir-fry onions, celery and yellow capsicum for 5 minutes. Add mushrooms and stir-fry for 2–3 minutes. Add cinnamon, salt and black pepper to taste. Return beef to the pan. Reduce heat and stir-fry for 5 minutes.

- Spoon beef filling into capsicums. Arrange on a greased baking tray and drizzle the remaining oil over capsicums. Bake in a preheated oven at 190°C (370°F) for 30 minutes.

- Serve garnished with parsley.

thai-style spicy fried rice

Unlike Chinese fried rice, this Thai version is fragrant with the addition of coconut milk. The chillies and curry powder add spice while making it distinctively Thai.

Serves 4

Ingredients

Thai fragrant rice (jasmine rice)	345 g (12 oz), washed and drained
Coconut milk	500 ml (16 fl oz / 2 cups)
Vegetable oil	2 Tbsp
Garlic	2 cloves, peeled and finely chopped
Ginger	2.5-cm (1-in) knob, peeled and grated
Chicken breasts	225 (8 oz), boneless, skinned and cut into small squares
Green chilli	1, seeded and cut into strips
Red chilli	1, seeded and cut into strips
Baby corn	6, quartered
Chilli oil	1 tsp
Curry powder	1 Tbsp
Salt	to taste
Eggs	2, beaten
Spring onions (scallions)	2, chopped

Method

- Prepare rice a day in advance. Combine rice and coconut milk in a rice cooker. Set to cook. When cooked, leave rice to cool before refrigerating overnight.

- Heat oil in a wok over medium heat. Add garlic and ginger and stir-fry until fragrant. Add chicken and stir-fry until cooked. Add rice and mix well. Break up any lumps with a spatula.

- Increase to high heat. Add chillies, baby corn, chilli oil, curry powder and salt to taste. Toss ingredients lightly to mix well and stir-fry for 5 minutes. Stir in eggs and cook for 1–2 minutes.

- Garnish with chopped spring onions and serve immediately.

pork, capsicum and shiitake stir-fry

Shiitake mushrooms and tangy capsicum add a delectable flavour to this easy Asian stir-fry.

Serves 4

Ingredients

Pork fillet	550 g (1 lb 3$^1/_3$ oz), cut into 2.5-cm (1-in) cubes
Cooking oil	2 Tbsp
Red capsicum (bell pepper)	1, seeded and cut into thick slices
Shitake mushrooms	120 g (4$^1/_4$ oz), trimmed and halved
Salt	to taste
Ground black pepper	to taste
Spring onions (scallions)	5, cut into 3.5 cm (1$^1/_2$ in) lengths
Corn flour (cornstarch)	1 Tbsp, mixed with 2 Tbsp water

Marinade

Sesame oil	2 Tbsp
Dark soy sauce	4 Tbsp
Sake or dry white wine	90 ml (3 fl oz / $^3/_8$ cup)
Ginger	1.5-cm ($^3/_4$-in) knob, peeled and finely chopped
Garlic	2 cloves, peeled and finely chopped

Method

- Prepare marinade. Combine ingredients in a mixing bowl and mix well. Add pork and leave to marinate for 1 hour. Reserve marinade.

- Heat oil a large frying pan over medium heat. Stir-fry capsicum and mushrooms for 2 minutes. Add marinated pork and stir-fry until pork is cooked.

- Add salt and pepper to taste. Pour in reserved marinade and reduce heat. Add spring onions and corn flour mixture. Leave to simmer for 5–7 minutes, or until gravy has thickened. Serve hot with plain white rice.

spicy chicken, chilli and galangal noodles

Zesty lime, aromatic galangal and hot bird's eye chillies are tempered by coconut milk, giving this Thai-inspired dish its unique and refreshing flavour.

Serves 4

Ingredients

Lime juice	2 Tbsp
Light soy sauce	1 Tbsp
Chicken breast	300 g (10½ oz), cut into strips
Lemon grass	2 stalks, tough outer leaves removed, bruised and chopped
Kaffir lime leaves	3, finely sliced
Coconut milk	180 ml (6 fl oz / ¾ cup)
Vegetable oil	2 Tbsp
Garlic	2 cloves, peeled and finely chopped
Galangal	5-cm (2-in) knob, peeled and finely sliced
Red bird's eye chilli	1, seeded and chopped
Green bird's eye chilli	1, seeded and chopped
Green chilli	1, seeded and cut into thin strips
Mushrooms	170 g (6 oz)
Dried fine rice vermicelli	85 g (3 oz), soaked to soften and drained
Chopped coriander leaves (cilantro)	

Method

- Prepare marinade. Combine lime juice and soy sauce and mix well. Add chicken and leave to marinate for 30 minutes. Reserve marinade.

- Add lemon grass and kaffir lime leaves to coconut milk. Bring to a slow boil for 5 minutes. Remove lemon grass and kaffir lime leaves, strain coconut milk and reserve.

- Heat oil in a large frying pan over medium heat. Add garlic, galangal and chillies and stir-fry until fragrant. Add mushrooms, chicken and marinade. Stir-fry until chicken is cooked.

- Add reserved coconut milk and rice vermicelli. Simmer for 5 minutes.

- Serve garnished with coriander.

hot pepperoni pizza

Simple to do yet deliciously tasty, this recipe uses store-bought pita bread, for a no-fuss meal that can be whipped up in minutes.

Serves 4

Ingredients

Pita bread	4
Pepperoni	225 g (8 oz), sliced
Pickled cherry peppers	6–8, finely chopped
Dried chilli flakes	4 Tbsp
Mozzarella cheese	225 g (8 oz), coarsely grated

Sauce

Tomato purée	200 g (7 oz)
Tomato	2, finely chopped
Garlic cloves	2 cloves, peeled and finely chopped
Dried oregano	1 tsp
Paprika	2 tsp

Method

- Prepare sauce. Combine ingredients in a mixing bowl and mix well. Spread sauce evenly over each piece of pita bread. Bake in a preheated oven at 220°C (440°F) for 5–7 minutes. Remove and keep oven hot.

- Top pita bread with pepperoni, pickled cherry peppers and chilli flakes. Return to the oven and bake for 7–10 minutes.

- Sprinkle mozzarella cheese over pizzas and serve immediately.

bacon and capsicum pie

This hearty dish of savoury potato filling encased in rich, buttery pastry will be welcomed at any dinner table!

Serves 6

Ingredients

Plain (all-purpose) flour	225 g (8 oz)
Salt	1 tsp
Butter	75 g (2⅔ oz)
Vegetable shortening	75 g (2⅔ oz)
Milk	2 Tbsp
Egg yolks	2, medium
Cooking oil	2 Tbsp
Egg	1, beaten

Filling

Onion	1, peeled and sliced
Jalapeño peppers	2, seeded and cut into small squares
Bacon	250 g (9 oz), cut into 1-cm (½-in) squares
Potatoes	4, large, boiled, peeled and cut into small cubes
Tomatoes	2, skinned and finely chopped
Salt	to taste
Ground black pepper	to taste

Method

- Prepare shortcrust pastry. Sift flour and salt into a mixing bowl. Rub butter and shortening into flour until mixture resembles fine breadcrumbs. Add milk and egg yolks and knead to form a soft dough. Cover in plastic wrap (cling film) and refrigerate for 30 minutes.

- Prepare filling. Heat oil in a large frying pan over medium heat. Add onion and jalapeño peppers and stir-fry for 2–3 minutes or until onion is soft. Add bacon and stir-fry for 5 minutes. Add potatoes and tomatoes and stir-fry for 2–3 minutes. Season with salt and pepper to taste, remove from heat and set aside.

- Preheat oven to 200°C (400°F).

- Dust a work surface with flour. Divide chilled dough into 2 portions, making one portion slightly larger than the other for the pie base. Roll out the smaller portion of dough and using a 1-litre (32 fl oz / 4 cups) pie dish as a mould, cut out a pie cover and set aside.

- Roll larger portion of dough out and line base and sides of pie dish, ensuring the dough overhangs the lip of the dish slightly. Spoon filling into dish and place pie cover over. Pinch the edges to seal. Brush with beaten egg.

- Bake in a preheated oven at 200°C (400°F) for 30 minutes, or until golden brown. Serve immediately.

NOTE

For a super time saver, ready-made shortcrust pastry is available from the frozen section of supermarkets.

chilli con carne

Tenderly simmered beef and jalapeño peppers in a rich, piquant gravy make up this immensely versatile Spanish dish. Serve as a dip, with tortilla chips or as a main meal, with garlic bread.

Serves 4

Ingredients

Vegetable oil	2 Tbsp
Onion	1, peeled and finely chopped
Jalapeño peppers	2, seeded and cut into small squares
Lean minced beef	600 g (1 lb 5 oz)
Paprika	1 Tbsp
Cayenne pepper	1 Tbsp
Ground cumin	2 tsp
Tomato purée	2 Tbsp
Tomatoes	400 g (14$\frac{1}{3}$ oz), cut into small squares
Red kidney beans (canned)	400 g (14$\frac{1}{3}$ oz), drained and rinsed
Salt	to taste
Ground black pepper	to taste
Sour cream	300 ml (10 fl oz / 1$\frac{1}{4}$ cups)

Method

- Heat oil in a large frying pan over medium heat. Stir-fry onion until soft. Add jalapeño peppers and stir-fry for 5 minutes. Add minced beef, paprika, cayenne pepper and cumin and stir-fry for 5–7 minutes, or until beef is cooked.

- Add tomato purée, tomatoes and red kidney beans. Stir well and bring mixture to the boil. Reduce heat and leave to simmer for 10 minutes. Season with salt and pepper to taste.

- Serve hot, with sour cream on the side.

pickled pepper and lemon-glazed ribs

Coated in a lemony, tangy glaze, these ribs are not only succulent, but tasty and tender.

Serves 4–6

Ingredients

Pork spare ribs	800 g (1¾ lb), cut into 3-cm (1-in) lengths
Corn flour (cornstarch)	2 Tbsp, mixed with 2 Tbsp water

Glaze

Marmalade	85 ml (2½ oz / ⅓ cup)
Pickled peppers (cherry peppers or jalapeño peppers)	4, seeded and coarsely chopped
Lemon juice	4 Tbsp

Method

- Prepare glaze. Combine ingredients in a blender (food processor) and blend into a fine paste. Set aside.

- Preheat oven to 200°C (400°F). Place ribs on a baking tray and baste with glaze. Bake for 10–15 minutes and reserve drippings to prepare gravy.

- Heat a saucepan over medium heat. Add drippings and corn flour mixture. Stir until gravy thickens and remove from heat.

- Drizzle gravy over ribs and serve immediately.

snacks & finger foods

chilli cheese muffins

Lightly spicy, these savoury muffins have an added bite to them because of the cornmeal used, and are perfect for a tea time snack.

Makes 12 muffins

Ingredients

Self-raising flour	480 g (17 oz)
Baking powder	2 tsp
Salt	1 tsp
Cornmeal (fine)	225 g (8 oz)
Cheddar cheese	150 g (5$\frac{1}{3}$ oz)
Butter	100 g (3$\frac{1}{2}$ oz)
Eggs	2, large, beaten
Red chillies	2, seeded and finely chopped
Chilli powder	1 Tbsp
Garlic	1 clove, peeled and minced
Milk	300 ml (10 fl oz / 1$\frac{1}{4}$ cups)

Method

- Sift flour, baking powder and salt into a mixing bowl. Stir in cornmeal and set aside.

- Grate cheddar cheese and reserve 30 g (1 oz) for later use. Combine cheese, butter, eggs, chillies, chilli powder, garlic and milk in a separate mixing bowl and mix well. Gradually fold in flour mixture until just combined.

- Pour batter into a lined 12-hole muffin tin and top with remaining cheese. Bake in a preheated oven at 180°C (350°F) for 20 minutes until tops are golden brown.

- Serve warm.

lime avocado pepper ice cream

Despite its unusual combination of flavours, this cool dessert is creamy and refreshing—definitely worth a try!

Serves 4

Ingredients

Vanilla ice cream	1 litre (32 fl oz / 4 cups)
Lime juice	4 Tbsp
Jalapeño peppers	2, seeded and chopped
Honey	3 Tbsp
Grated skinned coconut	100 g (3½ oz)
Avocadoes	2, pitted and peeled
Coconut milk	125 ml (4 fl oz / ½ cup)

Method

- Leave ice cream to soften at room temperature for 3–5 minutes.
- Place lime juice, peppers, honey, grated coconut and avocadoes in a blender (food processor) and blend into a fine paste.
- Spoon softened ice cream into a mixing bowl. Add coconut milk and blended mixture and mix well. Transfer ice cream to a container suitable for freezing and return to the freezer for 1–2 hours or until hardened before serving.

grilled capsicum tartlets

These little capsicum tartlets make a great snack as well as for a party spread.

Makes 24

Ingredients

Plain (all-purpose) flour	175 g (6 oz)
Butter	75 g (2²⁄₃ oz)
Water	3 Tbsp

Filling

Red capsicum (bell pepper)	1, cored, seeded and quartered
Yellow capsicum (bell pepper)	1, cored, seeded and quartered
Double (heavy) cream	4 Tbsp
Egg	1
Salt	to taste
Ground black pepper	to taste
Grated Parmesan cheese	2 Tbsp

Method

- Preheat oven to 200°C (400°F). Prepare a 12 or 24-hole tartlet pan.

- Prepare filling. Place capsicums on a baking tray and cook under the grill for 10 minutes, or until skins are blackened. Transfer to a plastic or polythene bag, seal and leave to cool. Peel and discard blackened skin, chop capsicum into thin strips and set aside.

- Prepare shortcrust pastry. Sift flour into a mixing bowl. Rub butter into flour until mixture resembles fine breadcrumbs. Gradually add water and knead to achieve a firm, smooth dough.

- Prepare tartlet casings. Dust a work surface with flour. Roll out dough to about 0.3-cm ($1/_{10}$-in) thickness and use a circular mould to cut out 12 rounds. The rounds should be about 1 cm wider than the tallest holes. Line the tartlet moulds with the dough and bake for 10 minutes, then spoon filling into each tartlet case.

- Place double cream and egg in a mixing bowl and whisk to combine. Season with salt and pepper to taste and mix well. Pour mixture into each tarlet case and sprinkle Parmesan cheese on top. Bake for 15–20 minutes until golden brown in colour.

- Serve warm.

vadai

Vadai is a traditional South Indian food that is commonly served as a snack and is best washed down with a cup of hot, milky tea to temper its spiciness.

Serves 4

Ingredients

Split black beans	300 g (10½ oz), washed, soaked for 4 hours and drained
Onion	1, peeled and finely chopped
Green chillies	2, seeded and finely chopped
Red chillies	2, seeded and finely chopped
Curry leaves	1 sprig, shredded
Salt	1 tsp
Ground white pepper	to taste
Banana leaf	1, large
Cooking oil for deep-frying	

Method

- Prepare vadai batter. Place black beans in a blender (food processor) and blend into a fine paste. Transfer to a mixing bowl and combine with onion, chillies and curry leaves. Mix well and season with salt and pepper to taste.

- Lightly brush banana leaf with oil. Place 2 Tbsp of batter and flatten using your hands. Make a hole in centre of batter, if desired. Repeat steps for remaining batter.

- Heat oil in a wok over high heat. Deep-fry vadai until crisp and golden brown in colour. Remove and drain well.

- Serve immediately, with sliced green chilli if desired.

capsicum and aubergine puffs

Tasty and fragrant, these little pastries will be the highlight at any party. They are also incredibly addictive—one is never enough, so make sure you prepare enough!

Makes 20

Ingredients

Egg yolk	1, beaten
Sesame seeds	to taste

Filling

Olive oil	1 Tbsp
Onion	1, medium-sized, peeled and cubed
Red capsicum (bell pepper)	1, cored, seeded and cut into small squares
Green capsicum (bell pepper)	1, cored, seeded and cut into small squares
Lean minced beef	200 g (7 oz)
Salt	to taste
Ground black pepper	to taste
Aubergines (eggplants / brinjals)	2, peeled and cut into 1-cm (1/2-in) cubes

Pastry Dough

Plain (all-purpose) flour	500 g (1 lb 1 1/2 oz)
Salt	1/2 tsp
Butter	110 g (4 oz), melted
Vegetable oil	125 ml (4 fl oz / 1/2 cup)
Yoghurt	250 ml (8 fl oz / 1 cup)
Egg white	1

Method

- Prepare filling. Heat oil in a saucepan over medium heat. Stir-fry onion until fragrant. Add capsicums and stir-fry for 3–5 minutes. Add minced beef and stir-fry until cooked. Add aubergines and stir-fry until soft. Season with salt and pepper to taste and remove from heat. Set aside.

- Prepare pastry dough. Sift flour and salt into a mixing bowl. Rub melted butter into flour until mixture resembles fine breadcrumbs. Add vegetable oil, yoghurt and egg white and knead into a soft dough.

- Divide dough into 20 portions. Shape each portion into a firm ball measuring approximately 2.5 cm (1 in) in diameter and flatten. Spoon 2 Tbsp of filling in the centre and fold into a half-circle to enclose filling. Pinch the edges to seal and brush with egg yolk.

- Arrange pastries on a greased baking tray and sprinkle with sesame seeds. Bake in a preheated oven at 200°C (400°F) for 20 minutes until golden brown in colour. Serve warm.

chilli pork sticks

This is a spicier version of the Vietnamese pork stick, a street food which can be found almost everywhere in Vietnam.

Serves 6

Ingredients

Flat bamboo skewers	12
Cooking oil for brushing	
Butterhead lettuce	1 small head, leaves separated

Chilli Pork Mixture

Minced pork	500 g (1 lb 1 1/2 oz)
Dry breadcrumbs	55 g (2 oz)
Red chillies	2, seeded and finely chopped
Onion	1, peeled and finely chopped
Garlic	2 cloves, peeled and minced
Ground cumin	1 tsp
Ground coriander	1 tsp
Chilli powder	1 tsp

Method

- Prepare chilli pork mixture. Combine all ingredients in a mixing bowl and mix well.

- Divide mixture into 12 portions. Wet your fingers with water and shape each portion into a rough oblong. Insert skewers halfway through each portion. Repeat steps for remaining mixture. Brush pork sticks lightly with oil.

- Place sticks on a greased baking tray and bake in a preheated oven at 190°C (370°F) for 30 minutes.

- Serve on a bed of butterhead lettuce.

spicy seafood mousse

This is a oven-baked seafood version of Thai steamed fish mousse, which is usually steamed in banana leaf cups.

Serves 4

Ingredients

Fish fillet	150 g (5⅓ oz)
Prawns (shrimps)	150 g (5⅓ oz), peeled, deveined and minced
Eggs	2
Coconut milk	200 ml (6⅔ fl oz / ⅞ cup)
Red chillies	2, seeded and cut into strips

Paste

Chilli powder	2 Tbsp
Shallots	10, peeled and finely chopped
Candlenuts	2
Prawn (shrimp) paste	½ Tbsp
Turmeric	1-cm (½-in) knob, peeled and finely chopped
Galangal	1-cm (½-in) knob, peeled and finely chopped
Lemon grass	1 stalk, tough outer leaves removed, bruised and chopped

Seasoning

Rice flour	1 Tbsp
Sugar	1 Tbsp
Oil	1 Tbsp
Salt	1 tsp

Method

- Scrape meat off fillet and mash lightly to break meat up further. Combine with minced prawns in a mixing bowl, mix well and set aside.

- Prepare paste. Combine ingredients, place in a blender (food processor) and blend into a fine paste.

- Add paste, eggs, coconut milk and seasoning to fish and prawn mixture and mix well into a smooth, firm paste.

- Fill 4 ramekins with paste and bake in a preheated oven at 190°C (370°F) for 15 minutes.

- Serve garnished with red chilli strips.

jalapeño cornbread

This delicious cornbread can be served with soups or salads.

Serves 4

Ingredients

Eggs	2
Butter	50 g (2 oz), melted
Buttermilk	450 ml (15 fl oz / 1⁷⁄₈ cup)
Plain (all-purpose) flour	65 g (2½ oz)
Sodium bicarbonate	1 tsp
Salt	2 tsp
Ground mace	½ tsp
Cornmeal (fine)	250 g (9 oz)
Jalapeño peppers	2, seeded and finely chopped

Method

- Preheat oven to 200°C (400°F). Line and lightly grease a loaf tin and set aside.

- Place eggs in a mixing bowl and whisk well. Add butter and buttermilk and mix well.

- Sift flour, sodium bicarbonate, salt and mace into a separate mixing bowl. Add cornmeal and jalapeño peppers and mix well. Gradually add egg and buttermilk mixture and stir well to prevent mixture from becoming lumpy.

- Pour cornbread mixture into a loaf tin and bake for 25–30 minutes, until cornbread is golden brown in colour. Remove from oven and leave to cool slightly.

- Slice and serve warm.

sambal eggs

This quick and easy recipe offers a great way to dress up plain, hard-boiled eggs.

Serves 6

Ingredients

Dried prawn (shrimp) paste	1 Tbsp
Red chillies	12
Garlic	4 cloves, peeled and finely chopped
Kaffir lime leaf	1, finely sliced
Cooking oil	5 Tbsp
Onions	2, peeled and finely sliced
Coconut milk	250 ml (8 fl oz / 1 cup)
White vinegar	½ Tbsp
Sugar	1 tsp
Salt	to taste
Hard-boiled eggs	6, peeled

Method

• Combine prawn paste, chillies, garlic and kaffir lime leaf in a blender (food processor), blend into a fine paste and set aside.

• Heat oil in a wok over medium heat and stir-fry paste until fragrant. Add onions and stir-fry until soft. Add coconut milk and bring to the boil. Reduce heat and allow mixture to simmer for 5 minutes. Add vinegar, sugar and salt and stir well. Add eggs and stir for another minute before removing from heat.

• Serve immediately.

curry chicken pie

Simple but delicious, these curry chicken pies are a must-try.

Makes 8 mini pies

Ingredients

Curry paste	2 Tbsp
Chicken breast	100 g (3½ oz), skinned and diced
Potatoes	200 g (7 oz), boiled, peeled and diced
Frozen peas	50 g
Salt	to taste
Egg	1, beaten

Pastry

Plain (all-purpose) flour	260 g (9⅕ oz), boiled, peeled and diced
Salt	½ tsp
Butter	125 g (4½ oz)
Ice-cold water	85 ml (2½ fl oz / ⅓ cup)
Egg yolk	1, beaten

Method

- Prepare pastry dough. Sift flour and salt into a mixing bowl. Rub butter into flour until mixture resembles fine breadcrumbs. Add water gradually and knead into a soft dough. Set aside.

- Heat oil in a frying pan over medium heat. Stir-fry curry paste until fragrant. Add chicken and stir-fry until cooked. Add potatoes and peas and stir-fry for 3–5 minutes. Remove from heat and set aside.

- Prepare pie cups, each about 5-cm (2½-in) wide. Divide pastry dough into 16 portions, making 8 portions slightly larger for lining the pie cups.

- Roll out each of the bigger portions to a thickness of about 3 mm. Place pastry over the pie cups and press down to line cups. Trim off excess pastry.

- Spoon filling into each pie cups, roll out smaller portions of pastry dough and cover each of the filled cups. Pinch the edges to seal each pie and brush with beaten egg yolk. Poke a small hole on each pie cover to allow steam to escape during baking process.

- Bake in a preheated oven at 190°C (370 °F) for 20 minutes or until pie crust is cooked and golden brown. Serve immediately.

mexican hot nuts

This version uses chilli powder instead of chopped chillies. These nuts keep for up to weeks in the refrigerator.

Makes 450 g (1 lb)

Ingredients

Walnuts	140 g (5 oz)
Cashew nuts or Pecans	140 g (5 oz)
Peanuts	140 g (5 oz)
Butter	4 Tbsp, melted
Chilli powder	2 Tbsp
Ground cumin	$\frac{1}{2}$ tsp

Method

- Combine nuts and melted butter in a mixing bowl. Toss lightly until nuts are evenly coated.
- Spread nuts on a baking sheet. Bake in a preheated oven at 180°C (350°F) for 15 minutes. Keep oven heated.
- Place chilli powder and cumin in a large mixing bowl. Add nuts and mix well.
- Return nuts to oven and bake for another 10 minutes. Leave to cool completely before storing in an airtight container.

glossary

1. Asam gelugur (dried sour fruit)

Dried sour fruit, or *asam gelugor* as it is known in Malay, comes from the Gelugor tree, a tree that is native to Malaysia. Sour and acidic in taste, this fruit renders a tangy, sourish taste to food and has often been compared to tamarind.

2. Banana leaf

Although inedible, banana leaves make hardy wraps for steaming and grilling food, while imparting a pleasant fragrance to the cooked food. Banana leaves are also often used as a serving container due to its smooth, strong texture.

3. Candlenuts

Candlenuts are traditionally used in Malay and Indonesian cuisine. Similar to the macadamia nut in terms of oil content, they are also used in traditional medicine for various forms of treatment, such as stimulating hair growth and curing constipation.

4. Capsicum

Capsicums, otherwise known as bell peppers, come in 3 common varieties of red, yellow and green. Due to their thick, fleshy nature, capsicums are suitable for roasting and grilling and are extremely versatile across different types of cuisines.

5. Cardamom pods

Cardamom is a spice that is valued for its highly aromatic nature and intense flavour. It is typically used in Indian cooking, and also as a spice to add to coffee and tea. Cardamom is also employed in traditional medicine for treating stomach aches, digestion problems and teeth and gum infections.

6. Cayenne pepper
Deriving its name from the city of Cayenne, located in French Guiana, cayenne pepper is made from the cayenne chilli, which is dried, then ground into powder. It is used to add spice and zest to dishes.

7. Channa dhal
Made of chickpeas that have been split in half, channa dhal is dull yellow in colour. It is commonly used in Indian cuisine as an ingredient in many thick, spicy stews.

8. Cumin seeds
Cumin is commonly used in Middle Eastern, Asian and Mediterranean cuisine. It is aromatic, with a slightly bitter, nutty flavour and is used in curries and stews. Cumin can also be purchased in powdered form.

9. Curry leaves
These highly aromatic leaves are used to flavour curries and rich, coconut milk-based dishes. However, curry leaves tend to lose their aroma rather quickly. Store in the crisper section of the refrigerator for up to 2 weeks or keep frozen, although this will also cause them to lose flavour.

10. Dried chillies
Dried chillies have noticeably stronger and more complex flavours, as compared to fresh chillies, due to an increased amount of natural sugars produced during the drying process. Dried chillies are typically used in Chinese stir-fried dishes, and for making spicy sauces.

11. Dried prawn (shrimp) paste
Dried prawn paste is made from fermented prawns. Its strong pungent smell and flavour is often blended with other herbs and spices to form the base for spicy dishes and dipping sauces.

12.

13.

14.

15.

16.

17.

12. Jalapeño peppers

Jalapeño peppers have a fiery taste and are commonly used to spice up salsas, dips and stews. The red variety is sweeter in taste as compared to green jalapeños, and they are also suitable for roasting and grilling. See also Pickled jalapeño peppers.

13. Kaffir lime leaves

Synonymous with Thai cooking, kaffir lime leaves are subtly aromatic and flavourful, and can be used in various soups and dishes. Kaffir lime leaves store well in the freezer.

14. Paprika

Paprika is a powder made from dried capsicums (bell peppers) and varies in range of spiciness and colour. It is used to add colour and flavour to dishes.

15. Pickled cherry peppers

Cherry peppers are suitable for pickling, as they are thick, fleshy and mildly sweet. In pickled form, cherry peppers are typically used in salads to add a tangy, spicy flavour.

16. Pickled jalapeno peppers

Jalapeño peppers are extremely versatile when it comes to using them in any sort of dish. In pickled form, they are great with salads, stews, sauces and dips.

17. Piman peppers

The piman pepper originates from Japan. It is a type of capscium, albeit smaller in size, with thinner flesh. Mildly spicy and sweet in flavour, piman peppers are usually enjoyed grilled or deep-fried.

18. Red & green chillies

Otherwise known as cayenne chillies, these are the most common variety of chillies. Red chillies tend to be hotter than green chillies, which are usually slightly sour to taste. Both types of chillies are suitable for use in stir-fried dishes and dipping sauces. Chillies can be seeded to lessen its spiciness.

19. Red & green bird's eye chilli (*cili padi*)

With a far higher level of spiciness as compared to their bigger cousins, bird's eye chillies have a bitingly hot taste. They are favoured in Thai cuisine for use in dipping sauces, soups and curries.

20. Split black beans

Split black beans, or black lentils, are highly nutritious and are commonly used in making thick, spicy stews (dhal) and various Indian flour-based snacks such as dosa and vadai.

21. Tempeh (fermented soy bean cake)

Tempeh is made from fermenting soy beans, so that they bind together to form an oblong cake. It is a popular ingredient in vegetarian cuisine as it is rich in protein and other vitamins.

18.

19. 20.

21.

Weights and Measures

Quantities for this book are given in Metric, Imperial and American (spoon and cup) measures. Standard spoon and cup measurements used are: 1 tsp = 5 ml, 1 Tbsp = 15 ml, 1 cup = 250 ml. All measures are level unless otherwise stated.

Liquid And Volume Measures

Metric	Imperial	American
5 ml	1/6 fl oz	1 teaspoon
10 ml	1/3 fl oz	1 dessertspoon
15 ml	1/2 fl oz	1 tablespoon
60 ml	2 fl oz	1/4 cup (4 tablespoons)
85 ml	2 1/2 fl oz	1/3 cup
90 ml	3 fl oz	3/8 cup (6 tablespoons)
125 ml	4 fl oz	1/2 cup
180 ml	6 fl oz	3/4 cup
250 ml	8 fl oz	1 cup
300 ml	10 fl oz (1/2 pint)	1 1/4 cups
375 ml	12 fl oz	1 1/2 cups
435 ml	14 fl oz	1 3/4 cups
500 ml	16 fl oz	2 cups
625 ml	20 fl oz (1 pint)	2 1/2 cups
750 ml	24 fl oz (1 1/5 pints)	3 cups
1 litre	32 fl oz (1 3/5 pints)	4 cups
1.25 litres	40 fl oz (2 pints)	5 cups
1.5 litres	48 fl oz (2 2/5 pints)	6 cups
2.5 litres	80 fl oz (4 pints)	10 cups

Dry Measures

Metric	Imperial
30 grams	1 ounce
45 grams	1 1/2 ounces
55 grams	2 ounces
70 grams	2 1/2 ounces
85 grams	3 ounces
100 grams	3 1/2 ounces
110 grams	4 ounces
125 grams	4 1/2 ounces
140 grams	5 ounces
280 grams	10 ounces
450 grams	16 ounces (1 pound)
500 grams	1 pound, 1 1/2 ounces
700 grams	1 1/2 pounds
800 grams	1 3/4 pounds
1 kilogram	2 pounds, 3 ounces
1.5 kilograms	3 pounds, 4 1/2 ounces
2 kilograms	4 pounds, 6 ounces

Length

Metric	Imperial
0.5 cm	1/4 inch
1 cm	1/2 inch
1.5 cm	3/4 inch
2.5 cm	1 inch

Oven Temperature

	°C	°F	Gas Regulo
Very slow	120	250	1
Slow	150	300	2
Moderately slow	160	325	3
Moderate	180	350	4
Moderately hot	190/200	375/400	5/6
Hot	210/220	410/425	6/7
Very hot	230	450	8
Super hot	250/290	475/550	9/10

Abbreviation

tsp	teaspoon
Tbsp	tablespoon
g	gram
kg	kilogram
ml	millilitre